The City with Horns

TAMAR YOSELOFF was born in the US in 1965. She is the author of three previous poetry collections, including *Fetch* (Salt, 2007). She is also the author of *Marks* (Pratt Contemporary Art, 2007), a collaborative book with the artist Linda Karshan, and the editor of *A Room to Live In: A Kettle's Yard Anthology* (Salt, 2007). She lives in London, where she is a freelance tutor in creative writing.

Also by Tamar Yoseloff

POETRY
Fun House (pamphlet) (Slow Dancer Press, 1994)
Sweetheart (Slow Dancer Press, 1998)
Barnard's Star (Enitharmon Press, 2004)
Fetch (Salt Publishing, 2007)
Marks (with Linda Karshan) (Pratt Contemporary Art, 2007)

ANTHOLOGIES
A Room to Live In (editor) (Salt Publishing, 2007)

The City with Horns

TAMAR YOSELOFF

LONDON

PUBLISHED BY SALT PUBLISHING
Acre House, 11–15 William Road, London NW1 3ER, United Kingdom

© Tamar Yoseloff, 2011

The right of Tamar Yoseloff to be identified as the
author of this work has been asserted by her in accordance
with Section 77 of the Copyright, Designs and Patents Act 1988.

Salt Publishing 2011

Printed and bound in the United Kingdom by CPI Anthony Rowe

Typeset in Swift 9.5 / 13

ISBN 978 1 84471 818 4 paperback

Salt Publishing Ltd gratefully acknowledges
the financial assistance of Arts Council England

1 3 5 7 9 8 6 4 2

A large volume of adventures may be grasped within this little span of life, by him who interests his heart in everything
— LAURENCE STERNE

Contents

Acknowledgements

'Concrete' and 'Field' were included in the anthology *Contourlines: New Responses to Landscape in Word and Image* (Salt, 2009).

'Tokens' was commissioned for the anthology, *Tokens for the Foundling*, edited by Tony Curtis and due from Seren in 2012.

Some of these poems or earlier versions first appeared in the following print and online magazines: *A handful of stones*, *The Bow-Wow Shop*, *Eyewear*, *Horizon Review*, *The International Literary Quarterly*, *The Lampeter Review*, *London Grip*, *Magma*, *Molossus*, *New Welsh Review*, *Poetry London*, *Poetry Review*, *Poetry Wales*, *Salt Magazine*, *Shearsman* and *Tate Etc.*

My thanks to Roddy Lumsden, for his careful and considered reading, and to Anne Berkeley, Claire Crowther, Katy Evans-Bush, Jenny Lewis, Rhona McAdam, Sue Rose and Siriol Troup for their generous support and invaluable suggestions. And my thanks as always to Chris Hamilton-Emery and Lee Smith at Salt for all their hard work.

The City with Horns

Part One *City Winter*

Concrete

There are no lyric dimensions
to its flat grey surface

no freedom in its hardness;
it houses many secrets

in its brutal expanse, provides
solutions. It is not charming

like daffodils or a pink tutu.
It refrains from statement,

turns its back to black words,
angry crows; it fills the bombsite.

It is not vulnerable
like the pale mirror you raise

to your face. You will fling yourself
against it, see what breaks.

Invisible Nearby Sea

This landlocked city

spills into suburbs, lots choked with weeds,
fills what space it can take

like the man sitting beside me on the bus
who's burst the banks of his bones to overflow —

we are too intimate in this folded space,
his breath timed to the beat of my heart.

I did not ask for his breath, his wet flesh,
his hands like slippery fish —

he must want to escape the swell
of his body, the contrived constraints of clothes.

And he will sense that I carry
the stagnant air of shuttered rooms, stalled lifts,

the slow creep of complacency. But still
it rises from tarmac to find us, clings

to our skin: that saline longing
for somewhere else.

Cryptographer

after Quattro Stagioni: Inverno *by Cy Twombly*

I string together little fables
in a language no one understands.

So much wounds me.
I write it down, cross it out:

a formula for contentedness —
instead so much violence.

They could kill me with a look.

You come to me in dreams,
blurred touch of your hand.

Your name scrawled on every wall.
Your shadow stalks me.

How we got here I don't know,
there is nowhere else.

Winter obliterates us, dizzy light,
our white youth.

Siberia

They are drinking tea from the samovar
and he is watching the steam
rise from her glass, the way her lips
flutter over its rim.

She takes from his outstretched hand
the tiny creature caught in amber—
the colour of her eyes.

She says, if you listen to the snow
it's like your heart shattering slowly.

The Russian Ending

We have no face
in the mirror, reader, we have no life
apart from the one you granted us
when you opened the book.

Turn the page. In the dead of winter, dead
of night, after a long illness, the last confession,
we release ourselves
to grief, a hard spring, a lost lover.

We ask you: what is wrong with our world,
with our hearts? Will we learn
to love again? Will we ever believe
in God, in redemption, in the parched earth?

Will our pain ever match
what happens in your world, where words
break on air like the rubble
of our homes? There is no end to it.

Reading *Ulysses* in the Teri Aki Sushi Bar

He would have liked the concentric circles
of the California roll, whorls of salmon and avocado,
brightwhite rice, the ginger fanned
across the plate—like Molly Bloom,
her legs apart—the saki hot
in his throat, a trill of syllables.

He would have admired my discipline,
my quiet journey with Leopold
and tuna maki—squintyeyed
over the page, the words
running away from sense.

The Dublin streets swell with rain,
delicate perfume of dung, and
there's a man hurrying home,
brown eyes saltblue, with no umbrella.
          I will know him, oh yes, by the shrug
of his shoulders, hunch of his coat,
the way he looks up, suddenly,
comprehends

                    that somewhere a girl, pretty,
captures a fishy gobbet in her chopsticks,
raises it to her lips, that first bite releasing
brine, bladderwrack, the green rot
of the ocean floor.
                    If only he
could sit across from her, worship
her perfect little teeth.

He will pass me on the street
one evening when the rain
smells like the ocean,

       flame memory for an instant
before we turn our separate corners,
pull our collars to our throats.

Shadow

Towerblocks cradle us like bookends:
I'm a slim volume, you're
leatherbound, slightly foxed.

The city loves us today.
We could be advertising
Ray Ban, *Ricard*.

Late sun casts us
as giants on the sidewalk.

Wish you were

Men are tearing up the pavement.
They unearth Roman bones, sometimes treasure,

sometimes just the dirt
on which all of this is built.

We pick our way through debris. I show you scars,
bombsites and brownfields.

You buy a postcard of boobs
disguised as cartoon mice, send it to yourself;

you were never sentimental.
You stare at skinny girls, with their mascara

and period clothes, their chignons swept into nets,
drenched in their own storm.

I know how they feel. You want to see
Cockneys, a coat of whitewash.

You have monuments of your own.

Mannequins on 7th Street

for Robert Vas Dias, after Anthony Eyton

We desire them to be perfect:
limbs without blemish, Malibu-bronzed,
robed in fuchsia and gold, smouldering
goddesses in a city leached to grey.

We, merely flesh, race past, hail cabs,
jump buses, never to strike
their timeless pose.

We must embrace the gift of the street,
the glare of chaos, of things being various.
The frail instant needs us to record it;
the mute made audible, still life animated.

They keep watch from their temple
of glass, stranded in silence, all dressed up
and nowhere to go.

The Sadness of the Scrapyard

A phrase used by Margaret Drabble to describe the work of the artist
Prunella Clough

A plastic arm, tiny fingers grasping
nothing. One shoe, the other
long missing. No attachments

in this corrugated space,
this ochre mound of loss
where things shed their colours.

To love the scraggy ends
is to love everything;
our heaven's a slab of ruin,

broken glass and scrap
piercing skin, heralding
rusty blood, cloudy courage.

What is hard we'll soften
with our shapes, what we see
indefinable in the heap

but still something gleams
even when all around us
is asleep.

Tokens

Objects which were left by mothers giving up their babies to the Foundling Hospital between 1741 and 1750 and which remained the property of the hospital governors.

1

My heart has fled,
its good meat
a nourishment for another

and what is left
is this case for nothing,
hard and empty,

a reminder of the mother
who carried you inside her
then released you to the light.

2

How can we be so beautiful,
rejected by our creator,
jewels born out of sand?

We grow to fit our conditions,
the mantle of our host
a temporary home.

We are firm, imperfect,
like grains of rice which do not
stave off your hunger.

Too dear for the likes of her,
your mother. A seamstress
or a lady's maid, fallen

from grace, the way we fell
from a bodice or a brooch,
our lustre dimmed.

3

I am a shield for a thumb,
in the bright battle
of needle and thread,

an old hat, a nip of rum,
a tap on the head
for the naughty child,

a shuck of tin, a tick
on the glass from a blowse
saying *let me in*,

a neat bit, a magic trick:
tip me and I'm gone,
gone, like the girl

who handed me over,
a tiny trinket, nothing
she'd miss.

4

I am a gaol without a door,
a will of iron. I cannot release
the circle of myself, latched

to my heartless body. No rest
from the work of obstruction,
no rest for those who've sinned.

I heave a weight, cold
to the touch, I taste of death
when you put me to your tongue

but I am speechless, charmless.
I am the warden of memory
and I have thrown away the key.

5

This to remember her by:
her profile realised in me,
the callous ache of shell,

each curl of her hair,
the noble line of her nose,
but she remains unknown;

a speck of a woman
receding, like my nature,
underwater.

6

to a door I cannot open
to a heart that will stay broken
to a story never told

to a Bible that holds your name
to a locket that hides your face
to the story of your shame

to a puzzle I can't mend
to a tear I can't unrend
to a story without end

Blackwork

A broken heart
Backstitched on a linen sleeve in black;
The dye corroded, like my love, the threads
Which held us worn away. You take your leave.

You take your leave.
I count the weary days in lengths of crewel,
Flowers wither on the bodice, the mirror lies.
I spin a gauze in blue, to match your eyes.

To match your eyes
To mine again, I'd give my own; what need
Have I of sight without you in my weave?
In my grief, the rose gives up the ghost.

Give up the ghost,
Devastated soul, and sing your last.
No fairings will he bring to show his love.
A black cockade I'll wear above my heart.

Stamps

Long after the letters they carried have vanished,
they flourish, unstuck from envelopes, edges
like stiffened lace, the watermark, a ghost of order.
There is value in error: the Inverted Airmail,
its kamikaze Curtiss printed upside-down,
the three-cent Farley's Folly, the Swedish Yellow.
They are prized, these rare mistakes.
But you keep even the most common for the sake
of completion. Strange princes, exotic flora,
clipper ships: all cancelled, their journeys finished,
their countries gone from the map, dusty on the tongue,
now news speeds invisibly through secret cables.
What you hoard is the old world in all its slowness
magnified beneath your glass.

London Particular

The ghost of my father
emerges from a doorway at noon on Piccadilly,
his hair just turning grey, like the London day
he's sailing through in his double-breasted suit.

No more than smoke and mirrors—
that's what the city does
with its alleys, its burnished brown wood pubs,
scrappy parks, towerblocks toppled to leave

a legacy of empty lots. Locations
which are lost, which lose me
in their ordinariness, the light caress
of a stranger's arm as I pass by.

These days I find the haze
growing thicker, all the things I can't remember:
names, dates, faces. The city renders everything
anonymous, disposable.
                    It happens too with age:

same age as he was when he first arrived,
war still clinging to these Blitz-rung walls,
piles of rubble and dust, bilious fog
hovering like an illness in the sky.

City Winter

There's nothing more beautiful:
a smudge of taxis and buses
crawls across the empty grey; a muddle
of faces—lovers, long-lost friends—
rises to greet you. The mercury drops,
darkness yields to streetlights, headlights.
The edge of your known world.

What you've missed—
hidden behind the bright dome
of a church, the slashed glass
of an office block, massed clouds.
Last greens of summer
still in your head, a sudden recollection
of heat—*nothing more beautiful*

*than knowing something is going
to be over*. You walk the streets, the map
ingrained in your feet, stare
into uncurtained rooms
lit and ready for intimacies—
you've been outside yourself
too long. What you want

you won't find here. A train
leaves the city, its complicated tracks
weave past buildings still to be built,
girders lifting beyond the horizon,
its passengers bound for those lit rooms
flickering like grubby stars
on the outskirts.

Part Two *The City with Horns*

Every good artist paints what he is.

— JACKSON POLLOCK

If Jackson Pollock tore the door off the men's room at the Cedar it was something he just did and was interesting, not an annoyance. You couldn't see into it anyway, and besides there was then a sense of genius.

— FRANK O'HARA

The city with horns

like the steer he claimed he lassoed out West,
all ten-gallon hat and heft, hugging the bar at the Cedar,

like a bull, great bulk of the Minotaur,
naked and erect, Europa bowing at his feet;

the streets of Europe choked with blood and dust,
as he wakes in a sweat from a dream of death,

horny again, no broad brave enough to fuck him,
this beast of a man, a real artist, no bullshit,

like the sax at the Five Spot or some
Village dive, a diva with skin like coal,

like the angel choir, cabbies leaning on their horns
as he trumpets down the Bowery, just the guy

to wrestle this city to its knees, *exciting
as all hell.*

Lee Visits the Studio

What beast must I adore?
— RIMBAUD

She said that we screwed once —
must have been drunk, she was so ugly
she was beautiful, her pogrom face,
its broad Ukrainian plains, sausage lips,

but legs that could kill a man,
a body that moved like oil on water,
sliding through the door
before I could kick her out.

≈

The work was nothing much —
sub-Picasso — we were all doing
that kind of stuff. But Jack had
something, a gesture, a freedom,

I couldn't say, couldn't take my eyes
off his huge, broad hands, worker's
hands that could lay rails,
bend steel, break a girl in two.

Those big canvases
filled with the junk in his head,
loopy birds and twisted women.
I guess I fell in love.

≈

She stood before *The Magic Mirror*
like it might swallow her whole,
her bird lips fluttering as if to speak,
small bird shoulders shaking,

she kept staring at my hands,
and I wanted to grab her, hit her,
kiss her, don't know what,
she had me so shook up,

she was like a cold jolt
of Russian vodka — straight.

∼

The real deal, more of a man
than those Euro poseurs, with their
waxed-back hair, perfect
manners, smooth strokes.

He'll wrestle me to the floor
until I'm black and blue,
leave me wanting more, throw me
out the door. I'll keep coming back.

I said *you're sex on legs*,
yes, he said, *I am*.

Springs

She taught herself to bake an apple pie
like a proper wife. She painted the kitchen
white—hallway, bedroom. Clean, bright,
new. He paced the rooms. She hid his booze.

She cooked his dinners, meat and potatoes the way
he liked, table set with a gingham cloth,
china plates, picked wildflowers to cheer
the vase, binned his gin. He threw a plate

against the wall, it smashed into a hundred
spiky scraps. Didn't want to be distracted
by the view, so he boarded up the windows
in the barn, locked the door. *No guests.*

Neighbours could hear them fighting a mile away,
both with mouths like sewers. She could give
as well as she could get. He called her *shrew*.
She threw another plate and spat

two can play at this. She banned his barroom
buddies, sent them packing back to the Cedar,
called his mother to whip him into shape.
A living hell, he said, and threw a plate,

threw the canvas on the ground and splashed
his paint. *A miracle*, he said, and raced
to show her. She gazed into his pool of rage,
Jack, that's a goddamn masterpiece.

Connected

I wanted people to sit still
for one goddamn minute but they
flash through your life—

       portraits are for the dead.

Trees construct themselves into a solid mass
as the horse picks up speed

see, everything's knotted
                together
the way notes on a staff spell music, a factory
churns out things, each thing
itself, but also a component.

How easy it is when density
unlaces, and you find holes you can
crawl through—
      light, a parting:

        Navajo bucks round
a campfire, dancing

if I half-close my eyes, I can make them
leap straight in.

Portrait of the Artist as a Depressed Bastard

His brow's a field of furrows,
his face half-cheek in shadow,
the night of the mind
descended, a silhouette of turmoil,
his cigarette mid-air.
Eyes too black, too deep,
and behind,
                the ghost mutt
tails him, the whistling
in his head, nature somewhere
in the distance, crusted,
tinged with sleep.
                    And still he's coiled
in the cross and weave of giant screens:
casualties, market shares, Burger King.

Short Voyages

for Jackson and Frank

         To digress
is to be alive and know a mind
at work, a body in motion,
the blare of the city, in all its
movements.
         No accidents,
only *cause* and *effect*, the future
which is not so dark but which
we cannot stop, speeding forward,
destiny at the wheel.
         Suddenly
everything is lucid, shining,
like children in the rain
or a lover, naked, and they
have to get it down,
         witnesses
to this age of flags and fear
where art might have a place,
sometimes right here on the street
or in a bar
         where men
argue the world into being
and drink to forget
tomorrow we might be gone.

Rebel Without a Cause

Lights. Camera. Action. Paint
whirls off the brush, as he drips
and dives:

GREATEST LIVING ARTIST IN AMERICA

Posing with his new Oldsmobile,
itching to take her out
for a spin, take in a matinee.

At the Regal lights dim
on the plush red, Jimmy's face
reels on the screen:

Once you been up there
you know you've been someplace.

The boy in Warnercolor, the boy
in the newsreel. Wheels
spun out, Porsche scrapped.
Like the magic trick, sawn in half.

The artist slumps in the row at the back.
He's seen this flick before:
I don't know what to do anymore.
Except maybe die.
                    Good trick:
exit stage right
before you crash and burn,
because tomorrow you'll be nothing.

Better to be a dead hero
than a deadbeat. Plush red,
lights dim.
                    You can wake up now,
the universe has ended.

Cedar Nights

Kerouac baptised the ashtray with his piss,
Rothko gazed into his glass, lost
in a haze of smoke (later he would slit

each arm, two razored lines, maroon on white),
while Gorky picked a fight with every guy
who strayed within his reach (his wild eye,

hangdog face, peasant hands, the dreams
he couldn't shake). De Kooning pontificated
over water (bastard) and by his lead

women shattered into pieces, all lips
and tits. Klein splattered the bar in black,
while dizzy Ginsberg's angelheaded hipsters

swore, and sang, and toppled off their stools,
then hurled themselves into the negro streets;
Frank was brashly erecting something new

from shreds of Rauschenberg and Lady Day.
And Jack? He was painting up a storm
(when he was sober), admiring his fame

from the summit of the Gods, until the night
she breezed into the Cedar, all ass
and attitude, looking for a guy,

and there he was, the prize, the mark, the Jack
of Hearts, the cover boy. She sidled over:
what's a girl gotta do to get a drink?

Singing Woman

after Willem de Kooning

Her flame of notes
scorches the bar.
Stilettos, lips, nails
in Fire Engine, Hot Tamale, Cold Blood.

Naked under the strobe
that dissolves her dress,
fires her skin, brings her back

from the dead,
from the flat white
of an empty room, out cold, blood
oozing from her lip:

the kind of broad you want to hit.
Floozy. Hot Tamale.

Violence finds her
again and again, needle stuck,
a groove scratched by
Camels and coffee, a gin too many.

One way
down; the falling scale
lower, lower, as her angel
rises on a puff of smoke:

what you'd call
a torch song, tremulo of pain.

Death Car Girl

*The nickname given to Pollock's lover, Ruth Kligman, who survived the
car crash that killed him*

I pulled myself up from the forest mattress,
one of those wailing women
of Picasso's that you loved, my mascara,
black bars down my face, the neck of my dress
torn wide, like your animal rage.

But I was safe, alive—to walk again
through New York streets, accepting the eyes
of men in well-cut suits and ties, potential lovers
beneath their clothes. You watched them
watching me—your jealousy pierced my skin.

I walk into the Cedar where their stares
cling to me like flies; I hear their whispers
rise to a shout: *death car girl*, *death car girl*,
loud enough to raise you for one
last drink. And she,

furious widow, who would tear my hair
from its roots, smash my bones,
weighs on me like the granite boulder
on your grave. I want to tell her,
if she would hear me out,

how it was: I was your Monroe,
your moll, your late model cream puff,
woman enough to make you happy
(your old clown face bloated with misery),
your rush, your thrill, your speed.

Night Journey

Sleepless, she rises from their bed.

Wet grass soaks the hem of her nightdress,
a ghost in the moon's
weak glow.

In the barn, that strange aura,
like he's hiding somewhere,
playing tricks.
            His huge paintings
cower in the dark,
unfinished.

Night was always his time.
Now he's gone, she claims it:
            everything in black and white,
like newsprint.
            She can't deal with colours:
Yellow sun, too bright. Red knocks her out.
Blue, like death.

She's tired of dragging her body
from one place to another,
hearing the sound of her own voice,
waiting for nothing.

Only her brush is alive, moves blind
over the canvas, no longer eye
guiding hand.
            Stupid to think
he might be here. He'd hate to be
some dumb spirit, all air and solemnity.

If he were a ghost, she'd know.
He'd bring on a hurricane,
burn down the house.

This is her own spirit — breathing, finally
free. Her hand grabs black
from the sky, her feet
stick firm in the dirt.

Gothic Landscape

And still, this dream,
the one I've had for thirty years:
dark knot of trees, pulling myself through
undergrowth, my arms and legs
slashed by thorns. Black like nothing
I've ever known

not even your knitted
blacks, paint spooling on the canvas,
somewhere beneath, a body, a face; not even
your tortured nights, bottom of the bottle
and no peace; not even my empty nights,
feeling the tangle of our bodies
that first time when you whispered
do you like to fuck?

And now I'm old,
my taut girl's body replaced
by a maze of wrinkles and folds.
A gorgon, a harpie,
awaiting death.

Until death, this dream:
I'm crawling, my knees
cut and bleeding. Blind. But I have to keep
going, I know you are here, I know
I am too late—what I will find is the
wreckage of your body,
blood flooding the ground.

I wake, the bathroom mirror
horrified by my face, its gnarled surface
a witch's hollow,
a haunted forest.

Alchemy

Guggenheim Museum, Venice

Just when I think nothing can move me,
room after room of Tintoretto, Veronese, Bellini,
the Virgin granting me her doleful eyes,
her pearly tears,

I enter a cool white palazzo,
find his huge canvas, which shows me the truth
of water and fire, in this place
of canals and candlelight, a city he never saw.

What he made was a world
in perpetual swirl, violent red, yellow bile,
the way the galaxy might look to a man stranded
in space, before science and logic takes hold.

And I stand before this picture,
the man who painted it
dead, like the masters shut away
in these palaces of art, their works their tribute;

wanting to pin beauty to the canvas,
dusty and flightless. But this picture lives, black
against the midday sun, legions of day-glo tourists
bobbing along the canal,

and I feel tears
welling up before I can make them stop.
I don't know why; I'm tired,
vulnerable in my light summer clothes,

he and I foreigners to a faith
which isn't ours: Christ on the cross,
the martyrdom of the saints, spelled out in
blood and gold.

Part Three *Indian Summer*

Forecast

The sky is cloudless,
reverting to its life before the birth of flight,
revealing no clues to its weather.

The track continues, dips
as the hill descends. I can't see
where it leads,

just the hills beyond:
green of nearness, parched brown
of distance, the far black

like the dark sound of the volcano.
It perches on an island unlike ours,
echoes in memory, a folktale,

until its people nearly forget,
immersed in the fiction
of their own lives, their small storms,

and then, in the force of its eruption,
it reminds them of their ignorance,
their blindness.

The wind bends the spruce
to watch their backs, as if something
has captured their attention,

carries the ash farther, farther,
like a whisper; I can't see how it coats
my skin, my lips, a thin film covers my eyes.

It settles over the hills, dusts the valleys,
furs the branches of trees. It catches
in the throats of birds.

Weather

You ask me how I know before the first fat drops fall from the sky. When I was nine I broke my wrist and all the kids in my homeroom signed their names on the plaster cast. When the surgeon sawed it off they came away too, forgotten now. I stared at the pale arm I'd lost touch with, like something dredged from the bottom, like the face of the dead president furred and flickering on the TV screen, like the first snow witnessed by the grandmother I never met, blinking in the cold sunlight of a new country. I feel it in the air, in the hairline of my bone knitted whole again—that ancient thing which will endure without me.

A Stone

I find it in the grove, a stone,
    among the rusted sacks of oranges,
        charred wood, its surface rough,

a piece of sandstone, sedimentary—
    the colour of almond, of shaded earth,
        the walls that cut into the terraced hill,

but breached, so I can see the glint
    of quartz inside, little diamonds,
        fluid gas forced to burst to crystal,

broken by someone's shoe, or a tool,
    the sort workmen here might use,
        primitive and sharp.

It traps the sun, like the crystals
    we hung in dormitory windows
        to grant us power and knowledge

or that ring—its surface swirling—
    a planet on my finger, which I wore
        every day one summer and then lost,

the way you always lose things
    which defy the need to own them
        and somehow make you sad.

I hold it to the light, an ancient world
    cracked open, like the inside of a tomb
        that hoards a secret treasure:

golden sun, the golden orange grove
    in spring, fruit already turning.
        I put it in my pocket,

a relic, like all those other stones
             gathered on beaches and on mountains,
                  even a black chunk of volcano,

which mass on shelves, fill bowls and drawers
             and jackets, enough to build a wall
                  to shore up my forgetting,

souvenirs of a collected life: people, random
             words, ideas; some, flinty cliffside shale,
                  others, tough rock to weather storms.

Train

The smell of mould, of permanent dark
as we lunge into the tunnel, a cold
I savour in this unseasonable heat
before the sputter into light:

a far field, a bonfire; a man
and his accumulated junk.
He swelters in the wake
of his destruction. Blaze, then go.

Facing the direction of travel
I'm beyond the pull of nostalgia:
the future is wherever
I care to disembark.

Field

A place without a name, nowhere
on the map, but there were poppies,

impossibly red, cartoon blood,
paper to the touch. They mouthed

death in the grass. There were trees
shading the ridge. And your face.

Now we crawl towards autumn;
the train leaves on schedule

without me, travels through
chequerboards of rape and maize.

Only the field is true, contains
remnants of our hair and skin,

defines itself blade by blade.

Wreck

The waves rise and crash,
Break its will. It will not rise and
Carry our bodies to another shore.

An oceanic effort. A lost cause.
It hoards its treasures, glittering jewels
Worn to grey, an empty case.

The Captain's log, its past restored;
Words catch in kelp, sink to the bottom:
Let them lie. Here is silence.

But the divers have equipment,
They dredge up relics,
Crusted imitations of their objects

Until it's stripped, a solid mass of failure
Among the little transparent fishes.
What more is there to say?

Après un rêve

The road reveals its secrets:
headlights seeking the here and now,
a piece of tarmac, its pockmarked reach.
　　　White noise
yields to easy classics, the soprano
basks in a minor key; an owl
tears the darkness open and fast
we brake to miss him; he lifts
free to a branch, stares us down.
　　　As we move forward,
we look back; private thoughts, grand desires,
the leitmotifs we carry with us, receding
from our view. We breathe the cool air,
wake from our dream.

Mud

after Howard Hodgkin

I see the scuffs and knots and bruises:
what a body takes.

The sea at night, tarmac road—
an obliteration, a mistake.

The Japanese master contemplates
the landscape from his mountain—

I clear the mud from my window,
wait for a revelation:

the antiseptic tinge of boredom,
silt of the airless room.

Now it's quiet, the memory
of spring behind us. Nights drawing in,

the tide is out, so when I walk
the edge of the shore my feet stick fast.

What a body needs:
the green warmth, someone to hold.

Honeymoon

Our suitcase rides in circles, holds
what we imagine we will need, guidebooks and sunscreen,
socks and smalls comingling.

In the moonlit lot we are struck
by the heat. We enclose ourselves in the aerosoled interior
of the rental, radio tuned to cheery zithers,

the theme from *Zorba the Greek*. We creep
through the city, untouched since the recent quake,
a forest of concrete and girders, climb

closer and closer to the moon, tiny villages
clinging to the ridge. A dog chases our dust
to the limits. His echoing bark.

The night gives us only what is before us
in the nearsight of the beam, the valley below
a solid mass of darkness, impossible

to gauge the depth of the ravine, the distance
from the coast, not so far on the not-to-scale map,
a compass point, a magical name, the journey

always longer than expected: our destination
a picture in a glossy brochure
where we will raise our faces to the sun.

Lemons

Leaves in shadow, back-
      lit, sun pooled, denied;
      new leaves

purpling to clasp
      their flower, flower
        bulging to fruit,

sour promise—
      pulp smutting
        a frosted glass,

a terrace, acid
      on my tongue;
        the rasp of wasps.

A storm clots
      on the horizon, ants march
        the parched footpath,

warriors, workers;
      rust of old iron,
        of blood.

A cloud muscles
      small drops of rain,
        cold drop

of lemons, puckered
      suns (more like moons), fizzing
        against the stone wall,

the woodpile
      rich with ants,
        heavy air.

We promise ourselves
      a memory of sun,
         buy the postcard.

The lemons are having none
      of it. They bask in their gloom,
         refuse

to be sweet,
      leave the residue
         of their sticky kiss.

Hour of blues

Cerulean so bright
you had to shade your eyes
darkens to this.

Faces exist in two dimensions,
pressed and glossy. They slip
from your fingers.

You love the furred edges
of almost-blindness, the stillness
as things close down,

give up to night, and just like that
you fade to black.

Where you are

The river bursts its banks,
spills over the map,
over names of farms and towns,
faded and cracked, the paper
eroding in your hands.

The stones you gathered
on the beach, the trinkets
stockpiled so you would remember
have lost their shine
torn from their source.

You had a mind of summer,
tarmac scalding your feet,
the red stain of the sun,
nothing left but a small pile
of ash, a fire

extinguished—a wound
in the ground. Everything
has floated away: trees, roads,
houses, a world of water,
colours seeped to white,

sharp light of forgetting;
the way he grows pale
behind your eyes,
loses definition, as you
let him go.

January

Sometimes he appears
near the little bridge, Titian blue, wings
like the silks of emperors, sharp
against the grey.

Not today. Today nothing moves.
You focus your binoculars
on a patch of pure white.

You have to be quick
to see him. Ready for anything.

But the sky is thick with cold;
we are slow in our layers of black,
words halt on our breath.

The high sound of choirs
as we drive by the church.
The month for funerals.

We write lists of things to do,
resolutions, lose them
in the great pile of accumulations.

A covering of frost on the trees.
A vast hibernation. We raise ourselves
from sleep, we are ready
for nothing to happen.

Jetty

after Peter Doig

You stand at the end. It is winter.
The water, slivered through bare wood slats —
brackish, dark — sways with the movement
of small disturbances,
                              the life
of the lake, what life there is
this time of year.

You stare into the flat expanse of water;
it does not give you back yourself.

In the middle distance, a canoe drags
its past behind it, the water
clears a path then closes. It leaves no trace.

Canada geese rise in formation —
a compass pulling south, a 'v' for *vagrant* —
their cries like children's laughter
amplified over the surface of the lake

                    and the mountains
shocked into whiteness through a muddle
of cyprus and pine.
                        Everything
dissolving   even as you see it.
The eye takes in
the canoe, already further, further
than you thought it could drift
in the brief moment you looked away,
              and the mountains further still.

Everyday there is less.

You feel the wood beneath your feet,
hard but pliant, bending slightly with your weight,
water rushing under you, the deepness
of the lake.
            You sense these things
altogether, understand nothing,
your mind drifting to a point beyond,
a nowhere.

You once knew how deep it is, how wide;
forgotten now. You've forgotten the names
of certain plants and birds.
You meant to buy a book, binoculars
to see through the trees,
black fences enclosing you in dusk.

It is winter.
The water would chill you to the bone.
                    There have been lakes,
reedy and lush in summer. There have been oceans,
wide beaches, there have been people you've loved
running along the waves.
                    There will be others.

You have forgotten so much;
the constellations your father taught you as a child.

The cold glow of stars, so far away.

You can't see the opposite shore;
soon it will be too dark to see anything
but you can't turn back.

        Something keeps you here,
entranced by the black lake, little glints
appearing on its surface.

Even this feels too vast, this small corner
of the world closed in on itself by the woods,
the mountains.
        And you are smaller still
as night veils you, makes you invisible,
a distant speck, like the stars; the canoe,
somewhere else, further along,
out of your sight.

Indian Summer in the Old City

Sun finds my face, so long in shadow,
drapes me in gold.

Brick softens to flesh, columns that framed our serious lives
are light enough to carry.

Pale boys shed their blacks, flowers
still in bloom.
                   How could it ever end?

No monument to mark those autumn nights,
pink flowers glowing in the dark core of me.

Stone retains its decorum, cold
under my hand. It will last.

Notes

'Invisible Nearby Sea'

A phrase from Samuel Beckett's *Ill Seen, Ill Said*.

'Tokens'

The tokens are 1. a hazelnut shell; 2. a string of seed pearls; 3. a thimble; 4. a padlock; 5. a miniature cameo; 6. a key.

'Blackwork'

A type of embroidery which dates from the sixteenth century. The poem is inspired by the textile tokens in the collection of The Foundling Museum. The form is a version of one invented by Roddy Lumsden.

'City Winter'

"There's nothing more beautiful / than knowing something is going / to be over" are lines from the Frank O'Hara poem 'There's nothing more beautiful'.

'The city with horns'

Jackson Pollock wrote the following lines in the margin of one of his drawings:

> the effort of the dance
> the city with horns
> the thickness of white

'Exciting as all hell' was Pollock's comment on becoming Peggy Guggenheim's protégé.

'Lee Visits the Studio'

The artist Lee Krasner married Pollock in 1945. Lines from Rimbaud's 'A Season in Hell' were scrawled on the wall of her studio.

'Springs'

The small town on Long Island where Krasner and Pollock set up house.

'Portrait of the Artist as a Depressed Bastard'
   Based on a photograph of Pollock by Hans Namuth that has become
   the iconic image of the artist.

'Short Voyages'
   The title and the line "the future / which is not so dark" are quotes
   from Frank O'Hara's poem 'Digression on *Number 1*, 1948'.

'Rebel Without a Cause'
   Pollock was a fan of James Dean; it was suggested that Dean might
   play Pollock in a film of his life. They both died in car accidents
   within a year of each other. The lines in italics are quotes from
   Dean's final film, *Rebel Without a Cause*. 'Is He the Greatest Living
   Artist in the United States?' was the headline for a feature article
   on Pollock in *Life Magazine*, August 1949.

'Cedar Nights'
   The Cedar Tavern was the regular hang out for the artists and writ-
   ers mentioned in the poem. "Angelheaded hipsters" and "the negro
   streets" are quotes from Ginsberg's 'Howl'. It was in the Cedar that
   Pollock met Ruth Kligman, who became his mistress. Pollock was
   eventually banned for tearing the door off the men's room.

'Night Journey' and 'Gothic Landscape'
   These are titles of works by Lee Krasner.

I am indebted to Stephen Naifeh and Gregory White Smith for their
book *Jackson Pollock: An American Saga* (New York: Clarkson N. Potter
Inc. 1989).